Easter treasure hunt

with Toby, Trish (and Boomerang)

Tom & Peggy Hewitt

Lots to do where you see this

Text and illustrations copyright © 1997 Tom and Peggy Hewitt

The authors assert the moral right to be identified as the authors of this work.

Published by
The Bible Reading Fellowship
Peter's Way, Sandy Lane West
Oxford OX4 5HG
ISBN 0 7459 3560 5

First edition 1998

10 9 8 7 6 5 4 3 2 1 0

Acknowledgments
Unless otherwise stated,
scripture quotations are taken
from the Good News Bible
published by The Bible Societies/
HarperCollins Publishers Ltd UK
© American Bible Society,
1966, 1971, 1976, 1992.

A catalogue record for this book is
available from the British Library.

Printed and bound in Malta
by Interprint Limited

Barnabas

**An imprint of
The Bible Reading
Fellowship**

All set to go

📖 Luke 9:51

As the time drew near when Jesus would be taken up to heaven, he made up his mind and set out on his way to Jerusalem.

Journeys can be exciting, meeting different people, seeing different things, even eating different food. You don't quite know what's going to happen next. You whisk through the countryside in a car, or a bus, or a train, passing through towns and villages and it's so easy — you just sit there. Travelling in an aeroplane is even more fun, flying high above the clouds where the sun shines all day and the moon shines all night. What was the most exciting journey you ever made... and what was at the end of it?

Jesus decided it was time for him to make a journey, a long journey. But there were no cars or buses or trains, no aeroplanes. He would have to walk all the way, leaving the sparkling Sea of Galilee and its cool breezes behind him, setting out along the hot, dusty road into the hills... and on to Jerusalem.

It wasn't going to be easy. He would get tired. Some people would be unfriendly and not even give him a drink of water. But others would need him and welcome him. There would be adventure and, at the end of it all, the most difficult thing he ever had to do — and the best.

As we get ready to set out on our Treasure Hunt we'll need to prepare carefully. Who knows? We might just find we're on the same road as Jesus.

On alternate days of our Treasure Hunt find the word in bold type — the first is today. As you travel, write them in the boxes at the bottom of Day 28.

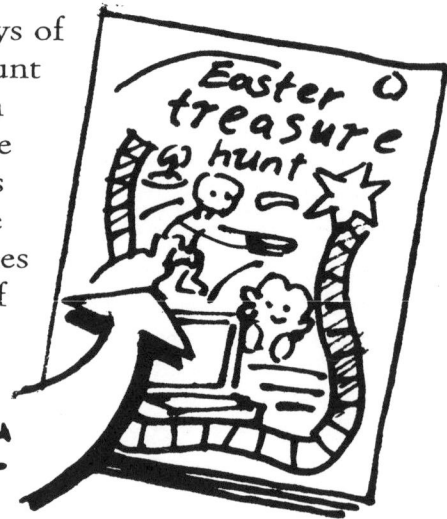

LOOK

at the cover of of your book. There you see the whole journey from Day 1 to Day 28 (apart from Days 6 and 7 which Boomerang is sitting on!). Notice the colours. Our journey starts by the cool sea of Galilee, climbs through the shady olive groves and then comes out in the blazing sun on the rocky road to Jerusalem.

I like your new clock, Toby!

It's a compass, Trish. We'll need it for the Easter Treasure Hunt.

Boomerang seems to know the way!

Treasure that will last

📖 Matthew 6:19–21

Do not store up riches for yourselves here on earth, where moths and rust destroy, and robbers break in and steal. Instead, store up riches for yourselves in heaven, where moths and rust cannot destroy, and robbers cannot break in and steal. For your heart will always be where your riches are.

What should we do to get ready for our Treasure Hunt? Pancake Tuesday — or Shrove Tuesday — is the day before Lent begins. For special times we have special foods... birthday cakes and Christmas puddings. Maybe you can think of others. Lent is a special time for looking at yourself carefully. Stand in front of a mirror and look at YOU on the outside. But what about YOU on the inside? How do you think and feel? What is really important to you?

On our Treasure Hunt we are looking for the most important thing of all. It will never get spoilt, will last for ever and will change us on the inside where it really matters. But have you got room for this treasure? At the beginning of Lent people used to clear their shelves of all the things that wouldn't last, and because of that, we still make pancakes today to use up the eggs and milk and flour which would have soon gone bad. What about your 'shelves', the ones inside you? Lent is a good time for us too to have a clear out of things like unfriendliness and jealousy, which go nasty if we keep them. When we clear these things away we can make room for the treasure that will last.

play dough →

✎ TO DO

Ask if you can borrow a frying pan. Put it down on two pieces of paper and draw round the bottom. Cut out the circles. Using some play dough, make a long sausage shape. Stick the sausage shape round the edge of one circle and press the other circle on top. Now you can practise tossing your 'pancake' in the frying pan.

The thing is to toss the pancake without it landing on the floor.

Well, that's all right then...

...it's landed on the dog!

Sometimes we need to be quiet

📖 Matthew 14:22–23

Jesus made the disciples get into the boat and go on ahead to the other side of the lake, while he sent the people away. After sending the people away, he went up a hill by himself to pray. When evening came, Jesus was there alone.

There's so much noise about — motor bikes, cars, aeroplanes, television, loud music, crowds of people. Maybe you like the noise... it can be fun. Shout a big 'YES!' if you do, whisper a small 'no!' if you don't. Whether you like noise or not, sometimes we need to be quiet — especially if we are thinking about something important like our Treasure Hunt.

Go into a room on your own, or into the garden if you have one, and just sit quietly and listen. What can you hear? Maybe nothing at first. Then gradually you hear small noises that you don't usually notice: the fridge humming, the stairs creaking, birds singing, water running. They're there all the time, but you just haven't been listening. It can be surprising what you hear.

There was once a man called Elijah who went off by himself to listen to God. First there was a hurricane, then an earthquake and then a fire. But Elijah couldn't hear God. Then there was a soft whisper. That was God.

Jesus loved being with people, but sometimes he needed to be alone, to be quiet, to listen. Try *to* do the same, even if it's only for a minute. Once you've learned to listen, that's another step towards the start of our Treasure Hunt.

☞ TO DO

In some monasteries the monks eat in silence. Next time you sit down to a meal with a friend try eating in silence. You'll both need to find ways of asking for what you want without speaking. No giggling, please!

Hi, Trish! How was school?

What's the matter? Aren't you speaking?

That *was* a sponsored silence!

Keeping in touch

📖 Matthew 6:9–13

This, then, is how you should pray: 'Our Father in heaven: May your holy name be honoured; may your Kingdom come; may your will be done on earth as it is in heaven. Give us today the food we need. Forgive us the wrongs we have done, as we forgive the wrongs that others have done to us. Do not bring us to hard testing, but keep us safe from the Evil One.'

I can remember, when I was much smaller than I am now, being lost. I'd gone shopping with my mum to the supermarket when suddenly, somehow, she wasn't there any more. Everything was strange and noisy and I was frightened. I was all by myself. I started to run, looking for her familiar face, when suddenly I heard her calling my name. She was there! And I ran to her. I don't suppose that would happen to you now, but can you imagine how it felt?

Imagine again: you are the pilot of a huge aeroplane and you're bringing it in to land. You can't see anything, only clouds, but the Air Traffic Controller knows exactly where you are and what you must do to land safely. All you need to do is to listen to his voice on your radio and do exactly what he tells you.

In the same way we need to keep in touch with God. That way we'll never feel lost or alone. This is the next step on our Treasure Hunt. Our Father in heaven knows just where we are, you and me, and what is best for us. Just talk to him as you would to your best friend. Listen carefully to his soft whisper and keep in touch!

👉 TO DO

Choose a friend and sit on the floor back to back. Give your friend a piece of paper, a pencil and a book to rest on. Now decide on something in the room for your friend to draw, but don't say what it is. Just say where to start drawing on the paper, whether to draw lines going up or down, curved or straight. When you've finished, ask your friend to guess what they've drawn and then swap over.

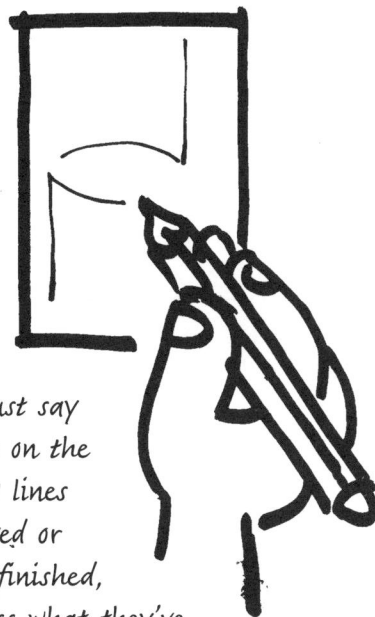

Trish, tell Mum I'm staying at school for football practice...

Fine, Toby, that's a double helping of tea for me!

Bother! It's just started raining — I'll be home on time.

Our Treasure Hunt is Jesus' journey

📖 Mark 1:16–18

As Jesus walked along the shore of Lake Galilee, he saw two fishermen, Simon and his brother, Andrew, catching fish with a net. Jesus said to them, 'Come with me, and I will teach you to catch people.' At once they left their nets and went with him.

Friends of Jesus...

Look out for them when you see this star — and then see if you can spot them in the crowd in the centre of the book.

It's exciting to get an invitation. You feel special because it means that somebody wants to share something with you. Or maybe they want you to help them to do something.

When that invitation comes from Jesus it's wonderful. He needs friends to go with him on his long journey. Simon and Andrew heard his voice calling to them and gladly went with him. Now he is inviting us too.

Yes, it's true. Our Treasure Hunt is the same journey that Jesus is taking. Are we ready for the adventure? Are we up to it? Jesus thinks we are. In the last few days we have been getting ready and now it's almost time to begin. This book is our map; it shows us clearly which path to take. And we are travelling with Jesus, so we can't get lost! When we say, 'Yes! I'll come...' we set out on a journey and at the **end** of it all will be our treasure.

👉 TO DO

Take a good look at this picture of the journey and see if you can make a model of it. You could use modelling clay, play dough, or even the sand in a sandpit. Shape the mountains, stick a flag where Jerusalem is and trace the road with a stick or pencil.

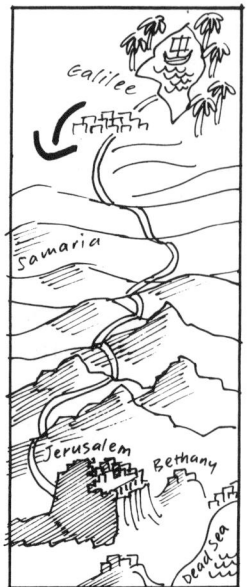

This map is just what we need to show us the way!

Where am I?

Travelling light

📖 Luke 9:1–3

Jesus called the twelve disciples together and... he sent them out to preach the Kingdom of God and to heal the sick, after saying to them, 'Take nothing with you for the journey: no stick, no beggar's bag, no food, no money, not even an extra shirt.'

Getting ready for a holiday can be almost as much fun as the holiday itself. Or is it? There are so many things we might need... is it going to be hot? What if it rains? Sunhats and wellies, snorkels and dinghies, beach balls and cricket bats... and that's just for starters! Then everything has to be packed and carried. Have you noticed that you often end up trying to persuade somebody else to carry the things that *you* wanted to bring? And what if the dinghy springs a leak or you forget and leave something on the beach? Too much clutter can be a worry and it often stops us enjoying ourselves. If we really thought about it,

we'd find we don't need half of it, anyway.

On our Treasure Hunt with Jesus it is important that our minds aren't cluttered up with things. 'What do I need?' 'What shall I wear?' 'If only I looked different!' 'It isn't fair!' Worry, worry, worry! Let's get rid of them so we can be free to learn from Jesus as we go. That's when we'll really begin to enjoy ourselves! It's amazing the things we can do and see if we aren't worrying all the time! Every day is new and exciting and different if we travel light.

👉 TO DO

Find a small paper bag. Now, imagine there has been an earthquake and you have to leave your house very quickly. You can only take what will fit into the paper bag, and it has to last you until this time tomorrow! What will you choose to take? Either put it in the bag or write a list.

Come on, Toby, we're going to have a lovely easy day on the beach!

COOL BOX

You're very special

📖 Luke 10:38—40

As Jesus and his disciples went on their way, he came to a village where a woman named Martha welcomed him in her home. She had a sister named Mary, who sat down at the feet of the Lord and listened to his teaching. Martha was upset over all the work she had to do, so she came and *said*, 'Lord, don't you care that my sister has left me to do all the work by myself? Tell her to come and help me!'

Did you know that, although there are millions of people in the world, no two people are exactly alike? 'What about twins, or triplets?' you say. Ah, well, they may look alike on the outside, but they're not always thinking or feeling the same. They are different.

This means that there is nobody in the world just like you — so you are a very special person. Which is why Jesus wants you to be with him on his journey — there's no one quite like you travelling with him. It was a great occasion when Jesus called in to see Martha and Mary. Martha started to bustle about making a meal, because she was that sort of person and she wanted to show Jesus that she loved him. Mary sat down and listened, because she was that sort of a person and she wanted to show Jesus she loved him.

Jesus loved both sisters equally, because they were both special people. And who knows? Perhaps when Mary had listened enough she would help Martha, who might then find time to listen to Jesus. Jesus likes us to help each other on our Treasure Hunt!

☞ TO DO

How many differences can you spot between these two twins?

Trish, you're supposed to be laying the table!

When the programme has finished...
I haven't got a plate!

There are ten differences.

The back-to-front Treasure Hunt

📖 Luke 15:11–13

Jesus went on to say, 'There was once a man who had two sons. The younger one said to him, "Father, give me my share of the property now." So the man divided his property between his two sons. After a few days the younger son sold his part of the property and left home with the money. He went to a country far away, where he wasted his money in reckless living.'

On our Treasure Hunt we'll need to rest sometimes and we can gather round Jesus while he tells us some of his wonderful stories.

Have you ever watched a video film being played backwards? All the little figures run backwards very quickly and finish up where they first started. In this story it's a bit like that. In fact, you could call it a 'back-to-front Treasure Hunt'. It's about a young man who set out on a journey.

This young man did all the wrong things — he didn't prepare, he didn't listen to his father, he didn't travel light. In fact, he took with him everything he owned. He travelled a long way and had a good time at first, but it didn't last and soon what he thought was treasure had trickled through his fingers. In the end he had nothing left, not even enough to eat.

Longingly, the young man thought about what he'd left behind and, because he was hungry, he thought about the food first. 'I'll go back home,' he decided. Off he set on the long journey back to where he had started. He was nearly there when he saw a figure running down the road to meet him. Surely, it couldn't be?... Yes, it was! It was his father. After all the young man had done, his father still loved him and wanted him back home. The young man felt ashamed. As his father flung his arms around him he realized that he'd found the treasure at last.

👉 TO DO

Take some plain card and make two picture postcards. Write one card from the young man in the story when he had just gone away... 'Having a smashing time...' etc. Then write the other card when his money had run out.. 'Dear Dad...' What do you think he would have said?

In somebody else's place

📖 Luke 16:19–21

There was once a rich man who dressed in the most expensive clothes and lived in great luxury every day. There was also a poor man named Lazarus, covered with sores, who used to be brought to the rich man's door, hoping to eat the bits of food that fell from the rich man's table. Even the dogs would come and lick his sores.

This is *the* beginning of another of the stories of Jesus that we'll hear on our Treasure Hunt. It can be fun pretending that you are somebody else. If you weren't you who would you like to be? A pop star? A princess? Someone on television? Somebody in a book you've read? Perhaps even a boy or girl you know who *seems* to have a pretty good time.

But have you ever tried pretending you are somebody you would *not* like to be? That's more difficult. The person at school who you don't like? The person who is helpless, or hurting and thirsty, or hungry and unloved? Can we understand what it feels like to be them?

Poor Lazarus, in an awful state, is carried to the rich man's door to beg for a few crumbs of comfort. But the rich man is too busy enjoying himself to stop for one minute to imagine what it would be like to be Lazarus, helpless, hurting and hungry. Why should he? Jesus finishes the story by telling us how the rich man later came to suffer himself. Then he realized how Lazarus had felt. But by then it was too late.

👉 TO DO

Make a 'television camera' by pushing the card tube from a toilet roll through the bottom of a cereal packet. Open the top so you can see through. Then 'film' the rich man sitting on lots of cushions, eating and drinking. Write a 'script' of an interview with him asking him how he feels. Then 'film' the poor man sitting outside on the pavement, cold and hungry. Interview him too. Get them to change places and interview them again. How different are your 'scripts' this time?

We're collecting for Oxfam in our class.

That's my last 10p, I've got nothing left!

You've got me!

Saying 'Thank you'

📖 Luke 17:11–17

As Jesus made his way to Jerusalem, he went along the border between Samaria and Galilee. He was going into a village when he was met by ten men suffering from a dreaded skin disease. They stood at a distance and shouted, 'Jesus! Master! Take pity on us!' Jesus saw them and said to them, 'Go and let the priests examine you.' On the way they were made clean. When one of them saw that he was healed, he came back, praising God in a loud voice. He threw himself to the ground at Jesus' feet and thanked him. The man was a Samaritan. Jesus said, 'There were ten men who were healed; where are the other nine?'

When somebody gives you a present, it's usually wrapped in coloured paper with fancy bows — it seems almost a pity to tear it apart to see what's inside. Sometimes, before you open it, you rattle it and feel it all over and even sniff it to try and guess what the present is. But it's important to say 'Thank you' to the person who has given it to you, even if it means writing a letter, so they know you're really pleased. That way you get to know each other a little bit better.

On our Treasure Hunt with Jesus we'll meet all sorts of people. Today we see Jesus giving the most wonderful present to the ten men. Not only did he cure their disease, but he gave them the chance to join in with their families and really live again.

Away they ran to be given the 'all clear' by the priests. They could hardly wait to get back to their families and friends. Then one of them stopped, turned and came back to Jesus. As he knelt at Jesus' feet to say 'Thank you' he was the only one who came close enough to Jesus to get to know him a little bit better. What wonderful treasure he found!

✎ TO DO

One small thing can make all the difference between being happy or being sad. Can you rearrange these sad words to make them say something important?

HANKY OUT

What small things could you do to make a difference?

What do you say? / Please!

What do you say? / Thanks!

What do you say? / Mmmm!

Jesus welcomes the children

📖 Matthew 19:13–14

Some people brought children to Jesus for him to place his hands on them and to pray for them, but the disciples scolded the people. Jesus said, 'Let the children come to me and do not stop them, because the Kingdom of heaven belongs to such as these.'

Jesus was very tired and when they brought children to him the disciples thought he'd had enough. They tried to send them away. But no. Jesus held out his arms to them and they ran to him. Why were the children so special?

Most of us are born with five senses — we can see, hear, touch, smell and taste. When we are children our world is full of wonderful things: we can see a ladybird on a leaf, we can hear the birds and the streams, we can touch somebody's hand, sniff the seaweed saltiness at the seaside and taste our favourite food. What is yours? Chocolate? Fried chicken?

If we're not careful, as we get older, we let ourselves get all tied up in knots... habits we can't break, worrying and thinking about nothing but being successful and making lots of money. We forget about using our senses and we lose touch with the things around us. Quite often we lose touch with God himself. It's like being half asleep.

While we are children, with all our senses awake, it is easier for Jesus to come close to us. That is why we are special to him when we are children. And he doesn't want us to be tied up in knots as we grow up.

👉 TO DO

Ask a grown-up to slice a little bit off the bottom of a potato for you so that it will stand up. Now, using drinking straws or cocktail sticks, make a potato Martian. Stick in five 'feelers' which can see, hear, smell, taste and touch. Make suitable ends with paper — for example, a trumpet shape for hearing, a hand for touching — and attach to the 'feelers' with sticky tape.

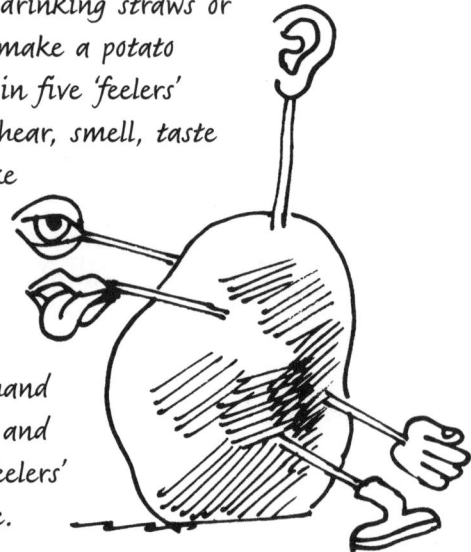

Ow! I bumped my arm in the playground! It hurts!

Have a sweet while I find something to put on it...

Don't make such a noise!

I can't help it, it smells so awful!

For the very first time

📖 Mark 10:46–52

They came to Jericho, and as Jesus was leaving with his disciples and a large crowd, a blind beggar named Bartimaeus son of Timaeus was sitting by the road. When he heard that it was Jesus of Nazareth, he began to shout, 'Jesus! Son of David! Take pity on me!' Many of the people scolded him and told him to be quiet. But he shouted even more loudly, 'Son of David, take pity on me!' Jesus stopped and said, 'Call him.' So they called the blind man. 'Cheer up!' they said. 'Get up, he is calling you.' He threw off his cloak, jumped up, and came to Jesus. 'What do you want me to do for you?' Jesus asked him. 'Teacher,' the blind man answered, 'I want to see again.' 'Go,' said Jesus, 'your faith has made you well.' At once he was able to see and followed Jesus on the road.

Have you ever thought what it would be like to be blind? No light — only darkness! Close your eyes and, with someone keeping an eye on you, move very slowly about the room. You will have to feel your way so that you don't bump into things.

Bartimaeus was blind. He could feel the rough stones of a wall warmed by the sun, but he couldn't see the wall, or the sun. He could feel the soft fur of an animal, but he couldn't see the animal.

Bartimaeus was good at listening and he heard excited voices saying Jesus was coming. He was sure Jesus could help him, but how could he get himself noticed in all the crowd? He used his voice and shouted very loudly. Jesus not only heard Bartimaeus, but also gave him treasure — light and colour. Bartimaeus saw the bright sun and the blue sky for the very first time... and he saw Jesus.

Let's pretend we're looking at things for the very first time. It's all new and exciting and full of surprises... just like our Treasure Hunt with Jesus.

🐾 TO DO

With your eyes closed, gently stroke your dog, cat, hamster or rabbit (or your friend's!) and feel the warmth of its fur. Now open your eyes and look at it as if you'd never seen it before.

Lend me your helmet, Toby.

Now I feel very safe on my bike — no more bumps!

If only I could have seen where I was going!

Taking a risk for Jesus

📖 Luke 19:1–5

Jesus went on into Jericho and was passing though. There was a chief tax collector there named Zacchaeus, who was very rich. He was trying to see who Jesus was, but he was a little man and could not see Jesus because of the crowd. So he ran ahead of the crowd and climbed a sycamore tree to see Jesus, who was going to pass that way. When Jesus came to that place, he looked up and said to Zacchaeus, 'Hurry down, Zacchaeus, because I must stay in your house today.'

Nobody likes to be laughed at. Sometimes we've said or done something silly, or maybe we look a bit different and people laugh — perhaps because they like us, or perhaps because they don't. Whichever way, it's not very nice and it makes us feel small.

Zacchaeus was small. People didn't like him very much because he collected their tax money and he wasn't very honest. He was really not a happy little man and when he heard that Jesus was coming he somehow felt that he had to see him. But because he was small and unpopular he was pushed right to the back of the crowd. How could he see Jesus? Then he had an idea. He ran to a sycamore fig tree and he climbed up it. He knew that people don't usually climb trees at his **age** and he risked being laughed at, but he didn't care. He had to see Jesus.

And Jesus, passing beneath the tree, knew he was there. Jesus gave Zacchaeus some treasure — he showed him he cared. Zacchaeus was never the same again. He was happy. He was honest. He had friends — and best of all he had Jesus.

Are we willing to be laughed at for Jesus? Not using bad language, or refusing to be unkind to others... Sometimes people will laugh and make us feel uncomfortable, but all these things are part of our Treasure Hunt with Jesus.

👉 TO DO

Make some stilts so that you can look over the heads of your friends. Clean, empty syrup or paint tins are best to use because they don't have sharp edges. Ask a grown-up to make holes in the tins for you to thread strong string through. And off you go!

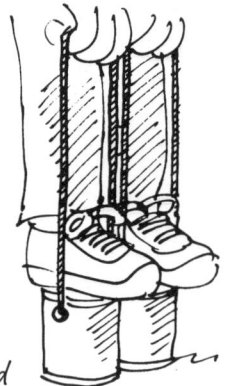

Do be careful, Toby...

I can see what I'm doing up here.

You see? No problem!

Jerusalem at last

📖 John 12:12–15

The next day the large crowd that had come to the Passover Festival heard that Jesus was coming to Jerusalem. So they took branches of palm trees and went out to meet him, shouting, 'Praise God! God bless him who comes in the name of the Lord! God bless the King of Israel!' Jesus found a donkey and rode on it, just as the scripture says, 'Do not be afraid, city of Zion! Here comes your king, riding on a young donkey.'

Here we are! Jerusalem at last! A lot has happened on the way and it looks like more excitement to come. Everyone seems to be in Jerusalem for the Passover Festival and they've all heard of the wonderful things that Jesus has done on the journey — our Treasure Hunt. People are even calling him 'King' because they don't like the Romans ruling their land. Some of them hope he might be their new leader. With everybody cheering him, how will Jesus enter Jerusalem?

When the Queen opens Parliament she rides in the State Coach, glittering with gold. But Jesus chooses a donkey. Although we're surprised, we'll join the procession, waving our palm leaves and cheering. But why is Jesus so quiet and thoughtful, riding on his donkey?

I'll tell you. A donkey is a symbol of love and peace, and Jesus is showing people that, although he's a king, his kingdom has nothing to do with soldiers and power, which don't last. His kingdom is to do with love and peace, which last for ever. What if some people don't want that? What will they do when they find out that Jesus isn't the kind of leader they imagined him to be? Look on the back of this donkey and you will see how they reacted.

TO DO

Here's a game you might like to try with your friends. Draw a donkey on thick cardboard. Cut another strip of card about 1cm wide and put some Blu-tack at one end. Now blindfold one of your friends and ask them to stick the tail on the donkey. Make a note of where they placed the tail and all have a turn. The winner is the person who has placed the tail nearest to where it ought to be.

Jesus had a band on Palm Sunday.

I don't think so, Trish…

He did! A band of followers!

15

Friends

All you have to do is: 1. Colour in the friends of Jesus as you meet them in the Treasure Hunt. Can you see who is missing? _____

_____

of ✦ JESUS

2. Can you spot some people who weren't friends of Jesus? Write who they are here. _____

3. Draw yourself in the picture. 4. Colour in the picture really well.

A super-market in the temple

📖 Matthew 21:12–13

Jesus went into the Temple and drove out all those who were buying and selling there. He overturned the tables of the moneychangers and the stools of those who sold pigeons and said to them, 'It is written in the Scriptures that God said, "My Temple will be called a house of prayer." But you are making it a hideout for thieves!'

The Passover Festival was the time when Jewish people remembered that long ago God had helped the people of Israel, who were to become the Jewish nation, to escape from Egypt where they had been slaves for many years. In the middle of Jerusalem there stood a huge temple and everybody wanted to go to the temple to thank God for the way he had helped them. But something had gone badly wrong.

Have you ever been to a supermarket just before Christmas? It's noisy and crowded with everybody jostling and looking fed up and tired. Well, *the* temple in Jerusalem was just like that; full of jostling and noise.

You see, the temple courtyards were full of people exchanging their money for temple money so that they could buy pigeons to take into the temple as a way of saying 'thank you' or 'sorry' to God. The trouble was that the moneychangers and the people who sold the small birds were very greedy and used the people's devotion to God as a way of making a lot of money.

When Jesus went into the temple to pray there was so much noise and jostling that God had been forgotten. Jesus saw how greedy people had become and he was very angry indeed. On our Treasure Hunt we are finding out that Jesus' kingdom of love and peace doesn't mean sitting back and watching when people are greedy and forget all about God. As you can see, Jesus did something about it.

🖅 TO DO

Think carefully what you would like to find in a church and write a shopping list. It could have things like 'friendliness, nice music and quietness' on it. What else can you think of?

No, Trish, don't take that tin of beans...

...from the bottom!

CRASH!

BAKED BEANS

The precious gift

📖 Matthew 26:6–10

Jesus was in Bethany at the house of Simon, a man who had suffered from a dreaded skin disease. While Jesus was eating, a woman came to him with an alabaster jar filled with an expensive perfume, which she poured on his head. The disciples saw this and became angry. 'Why all this waste?' they asked. 'This perfume could have been sold for a large amount and the money given to the poor!' Jesus knew what they were saying, so he said to them, 'Why are you bothering this woman? It is a fine and beautiful thing that she has done for me.'

There are lots of ways we can show that we love somebody — a smile, remembering someone's birthday, doing something to please them, or not doing something that would make them unhappy. I'm sure you can think of lots of other ways. Now, think of somebody that you love and just one way you can show them you do. Better still — go and do it!

We are getting closer to our Treasure. It is just before the day of the Passover Festival and Jesus is staying in Bethany, a little village just outside Jerusalem, when something rather strange happens. What is the most valuable thing that you have? For the woman who came to Jesus it was a bottle of perfume. Although the disciples thought it was a dreadful waste, Jesus was glad she had shown her love for him in her own way. It wasn't the value of the perfume, but what she had done with it and why she had done it that was important to him.

On our Treasure Hunt we are starting to learn what love is. It is not just about giving 'things' but about giving our thoughts, our time — and sometimes even more. We'll find out what love is really like before we reach our Treasure.

TO DO

In Greece people often give you a leaf of mint or some other nice-smelling herb. If you have a garden you could ask a grown-up to help you find a nice-smelling leaf to give to your friend or someone in your family. You could use dried herbs wrapped in a piece of tissue paper if you don't have fresh leaves.

A very special meal

📖 Matthew 26:20 & Luke 22:17–19

When it was evening, Jesus and the twelve disciples sat down to eat... Then Jesus took a cup, gave thanks to God, and said, 'Take this and share it among yourselves...' Then he took a piece of bread, gave thanks to God, broke it, and gave it to them, saying, 'This is my body, which is given for you. Do this in memory of me.'

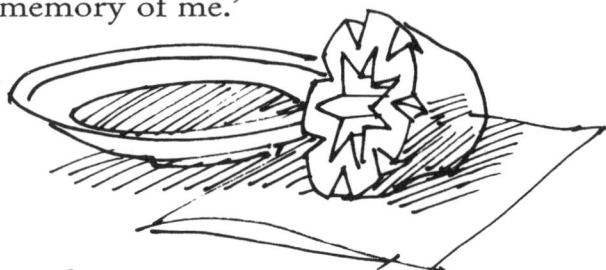

Sitting in front of the television with a plate of pizza or sausages and chips on our knee and munching as we watch our favourite programme is sometimes a great idea. Sometimes — but not always. Because this way we're really only having half a meal. The best meals are when we get together with our family or friends round a table, or at a picnic or barbecue and talk to each other as we eat. That's what meals are really all about. As we eat we get to know each other a little bit better. On all the important occasions — a birthday, a wedding, special visitors at home or at church — we eat and talk together.

Like everybody in Jerusalem, Jesus and his friends sat down to a Passover meal. As we are travelling with them, we can be there too. It is a very special meal and Jesus is talking to us. He takes up the bread and wine and, as he gives it to us, asks us to remember him. Oh no! He can't mean he's leaving us! Not before the end of the journey, the end of our Treasure Hunt! How *will* we manage without him? Everybody is looking sad, particularly Jesus. He seems to know something dreadful is going to happen... and we can do nothing to prevent it.

In our churches we remember this special meal that Jesus ate with his disciples. We remember what he said and did and we take part in it together, all over again.

👉 TO DO

Make a meal special by printing your own paper napkins. Ask a grown-up to cut a potato in half for you and carefully cut pieces out of the edge and make some holes in the middle to make a pattern. Put some paint into a saucer and print the 'blocks' on to pieces of thin paper.

The last day of the holidays.

When I have a hot dog and Coke again I shall remember today.

It's not easy

📖 Mark 14:32–36

They came to a place called Gethsemane, and Jesus said to his disciples, 'Sit here while I pray.' He took Peter, James, and John with him. Distress and anguish came over him, and he said to them, 'The sorrow in my heart is so great that it almost crushes me. Stay here and keep watch.' He went a little farther on, threw himself on the ground, and prayed that, if possible, he might not have to go through that time of suffering. 'Father,' he prayed, 'my Father! All things are possible for you. Take this cup of suffering away from me. Yet not what I want, but what you want.'

Have you ever had something very difficult to do and it's made you feel dreadful? Perhaps you have to do something for somebody and you don't think you can, or it will make a mess of all your plans. Or you have to take a test or an exam and you're worried in case you don't pass. Or maybe you have to apologize to somebody you don't like. Can you think of a time like that?

You just want somebody to come along and say, 'It's OK. You don't have to do it if you feel like that.' Or you wish you could wake up and find it's all been a bad dream.

Jesus was feeling like that. He knew how difficult it was going to be to do the thing he had to do, but he also knew, deep down, that he had to do it. In the end he put his trust in his heavenly Father. He was ready.

On our Treasure Hunt we are learning that our heavenly Father knows what we are able to do. And he will help us to do it — even when it is not easy for us.

🖐 TO DO

It's time to make another list. On a piece of paper write down one side all the things you like doing best. Then down the other side write the things you ought to do but have been putting off. Don't show your lists to anybody, but say a 'thank you' prayer to God for the things you like doing, and ask him to help you to do the other things.

What's up, Trish?

I've got to go to my piano lesson and I can't do it.

SOB SOB

Later...

That was easy! My fingers were just stuck together!

The impossible happens!

📖 Matthew 27:1–2, 15 & 20–22

Early in the morning all the chief priests and the elders made their plans against Jesus to put him to death. They put him in chains, led him off, and handed him over to Pilate, the Roman governor... At every Passover Festival the Roman governor was in the habit of setting free any one prisoner the crowd asked for... The chief priests and the elders persuaded the crowd to ask Pilate to set Barabbas free and have Jesus put to death. But Pilate asked the crowd, 'Which one of these two do you want me to set free for you?' 'Barabbas!' they answered. 'What, then, shall I do with Jesus called the Messiah?' Pilate asked them. 'Crucify him!' they all answered.

How could the crowd call for Jesus to die after all the kind things he had done? He had listened to them, told them wonderful stories, made them better and taken away their unhappiness. He never did anything wrong, but it had all come to this. Why?

Joiners and carpenters sometimes use some lovely old-fashioned words when they're given a piece of furniture to be mended. They say, 'Yes, *I* can make it good.' They mean they can strengthen the bits that are wobbly and replace the bits that won't last and turn it into what it was meant to be — strong and whole and beautiful.

Could it be that Jesus knew all about the wobbly bits and things that won't last *inside us*? Jesus, the carpenter from Nazareth, knew the difficult thing he had to do. He had to die 'to make us good' so that when our heavenly Father looks at us he'll see us strong and whole and beautiful, just as he meant us to be. As he stands there before the crowd we feel sad and heavy-hearted and even the day turns into night as he dies on the cross. But our Treasure Hunt isn't over yet...

👉 TO DO

Make a cross out of thick card — you could use an empty cereal packet. Measure each square carefully to make sure they are all equal. Keep the cross by your bed until tomorrow.

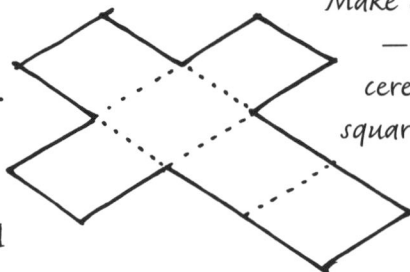

How much does Jesus love me? So much?

More than that!

You mean, so much?

What will happen now?

📖 Luke 23:50–56

There was a man named Joseph from Arimathea, a town in Judea... He went into the presence of Pilate and asked for the body of Jesus. Then he took the body down, wrapped it in a linen sheet, and placed it in a tomb which had been dug out of solid rock and which had never been used. It was Friday, and the Sabbath was about to begin. The women who had followed Jesus from Galilee went with Joseph and saw the tomb and how Jesus' body was placed in it. Then they went back home and prepared the spices and perfumes for the body. On the Sabbath they rested, as the Law commanded.

When someone you love isn't there any more you feel sad. You remember their face and their voice, you touch the things they've used and think about what you've done together. You miss them. It's a very difficult time and it seems as though the world has come to an end. And what about tomorrow...?

The day after Jesus died is the Jewish Sabbath and nobody is allowed to work or really do anything. So all we can do is sit and wait. We are waiting with the women for the Sabbath to pass...

We're all mixed up inside. We're sad because Jesus is lying in a tomb like a prison and there wasn't even time to bury him properly because of the Sabbath rules. We're frightened in case the soldiers come for us too because we've been seen with Jesus. We're lost because Jesus was always there, helping, teaching, leading the way and now we don't know what to do. And what about our Treasure Hunt? We keep trying to remember the things that Jesus said and did and wish we'd taken more notice. If only... if only... And what about tomorrow?

👉 TO DO

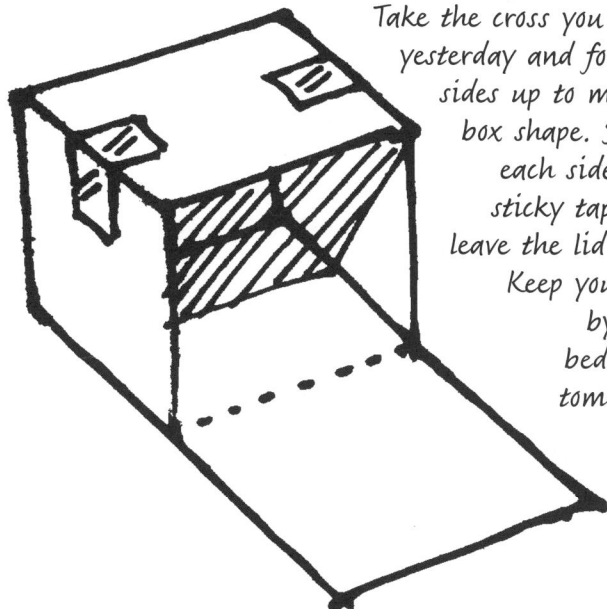

Take the cross you made yesterday and fold the sides up to make a box shape. Secure each side with sticky tape but leave the lid open. Keep your box by your bed until tomorrow.

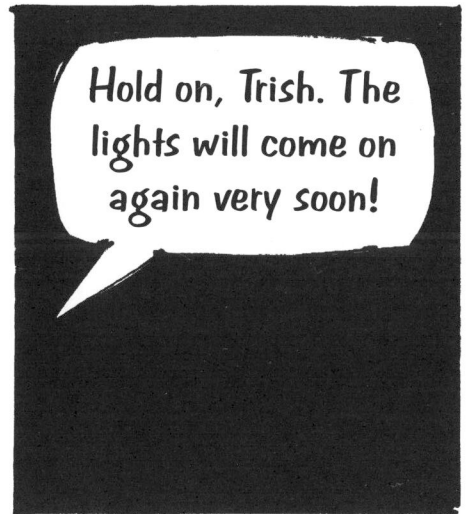

Where are you, Toby?

It's a powercut.

Hold on, Trish. The lights will come on again very soon!

Wonder of wonders

📖 Luke 24:1–6

Very early on Sunday morning, the women went to the tomb, carrying the spices they had prepared. They found the stone rolled away from the entrance to the tomb, so they went in; but they did not find the body of the Lord Jesus. They stood there puzzled about this, when suddenly two men in bright shining clothes stood by them. Full of fear, the women bowed down to the ground, as the men said to them, 'Why are you looking among the dead for one who is alive? He is not here; he has been raised.'

Spring is a wonderful time of year. Trees that looked dead suddenly sprout new leaves, blossoms and flowers appear, the sun gets warmer and the daylight lasts longer. Everything seems to sparkle with newness. I'm sure you've noticed lots of other things in Spring.

And those birds! Have **you** ever heard such happy singing? They're busy too, flying with beaks full of straw and moss, building nests, preparing for a big event. Suddenly there are eggs in the nest — but what are they? They just look like little rounded stones — until crack... wriggle... blink... a baby bird, a new life, comes out of the lifeless looking egg.

That's why, at Easter, we give each other eggs — to remind us of what happened on that first Easter Day. But Easter eggs are not our Treasure; just be patient!

Jesus' life was really a preparation for a big event and the time he spent in the stone tomb was part of that preparation. And then — wonder of wonders — the tomb is empty and we discover that Jesus is no longer dead! At first our minds can't get used to the idea. What an amazing Treasure Hunt!

This caterpillar doesn't look very well...

Oh dear, it's gone all crusty and dead!

I don't believe it!

Decorated Easter Eggs

(Get a grown-up to help)

You will need: unboiled eggs, onion skins, small pots of hot water dye, a few porous decorative leaves (e.g. primula, lupin etc.), 20 cm square of white cotton per egg, an old pan, strong thread. Lay the onion skin in the centre of the cotton square, put the leaves on top, then the egg. Fold the cloth into a parcel, with the onion and leaves next to the egg. Twine the thread round and round the parcel so that everything is held firmly in place. Put enough cold water in the pan to cover the eggs well and dip each parcel into the pan to thoroughly wet it. Sprinkle the parcels with dye, put back into the pan and boil for 20 to 25 minutes. Carefully life the parcels out of the pan and allow to cool. Unwrap for a lovely surprise!

Put your favourite egg in your box and give it to someone special.

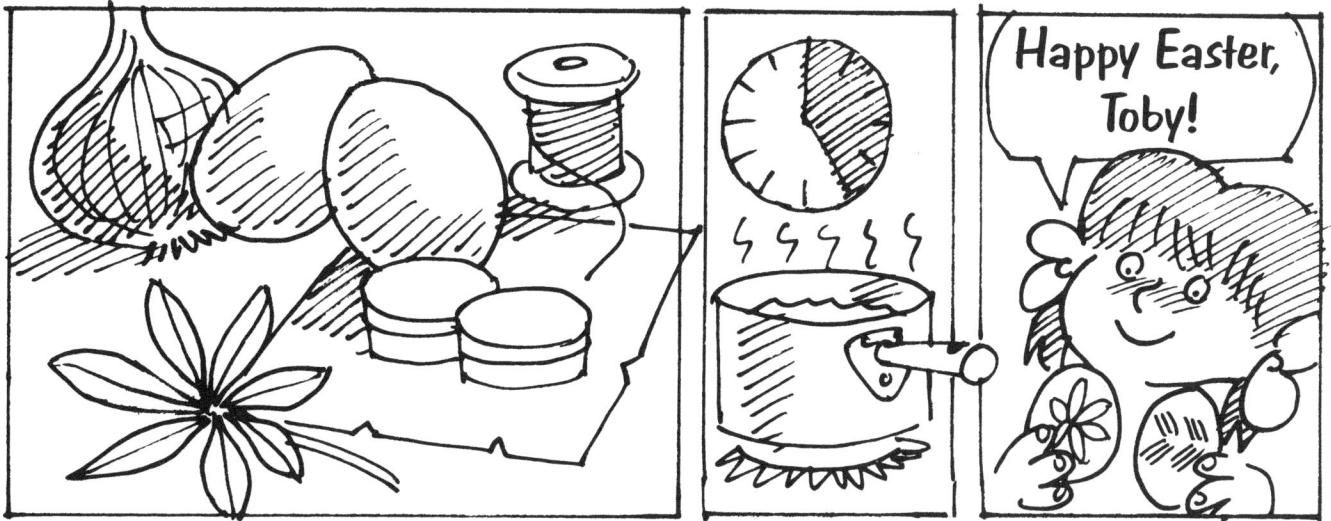

Happy Easter, Toby!

How to make your computer model

Carefully remove the back cover from this book and cut out along all the thick black lines using pointed scissors — you might need a grown-up to help you with this. Don't forget the thick black lines around the donkey, Toby and Trish and the bird. Fold firmly along the dotted lines with the colour inside the box. 'Pop-up' the donkey, bird and Toby and Trish. Carefully tuck in the flaps.

It really is Jesus

📖 John 20:14–17

Then Mary turned round and saw Jesus standing there, but she did not know that it was Jesus. 'Woman, why are you crying?' Jesus asked her. 'Who is it that you are looking for?' She thought he was the gardener, so she said to him, 'If you took him away, sir, tell me where you have put him, and I will go and get him.' Jesus said to her, 'Mary!' She turned towards him and said in Hebrew, 'Rabboni!' (This means 'Teacher'.)

Have you ever had a bad time when nothing seems right? You don't understand what's going on and what you really want to do is go away and hide somewhere. Maybe you've gone to a different school, or moved house, or there have been changes in your family. Then suddenly it all comes right. For a while you're still mixed up inside because you can't believe, at first, that things are going to be better from now on.

Mary was feeling like that on that Easter morning. So much had happened. She thought that everything she'd known and loved was gone and she was miserable. She wasn't expecting anything wonderful so she didn't recognize it when it happened. Because Jesus loved her he knew what the matter was, but he asked her so she could pour out her troubles. Then it would be easier for her to see things as they really were.

In the midst of her tears Jesus only needed to say one word, 'Mary'. He spoke her name and immediately she knew that it was Jesus standing there.

Jesus understands our troubles. When we feel unhappy inside he'll wipe away our tears and speak softly to us, too.

✎ TO DO

Next time you are together in one room with your family or friends try spreading a little happiness. Here's how: putting as much happiness as you can into your voice say to the person sitting next to you, 'Have you heard?' They reply, 'No, what?' Still sounding happy, you then both ask somebody else the same question, and so on round the room. It's amazing to feel the buzz of joy and excitement that fills the room!

What do you call a lamb without legs?

A cloud!

26

A walk with Jesus

📖 Luke 24:13–16 & 28–31

On that same day two of Jesus' followers were going to a village named Emmaus, about eleven kilometres from Jerusalem, and they were talking to each other about all the things that had happened. As they talked and discussed, Jesus himself drew near and walked along with them; they saw him, but somehow did not recognize him... As they came near the village to which they were going, Jesus acted as if he were going farther; but they held him back, saying, 'Stay with us...' He sat down to eat with them, took the bread, and said the blessing; then he broke the bread and gave it to them. Then their eyes were opened and they recognized him, but he disappeared from their sight.

In Jerusalem in the days of Jesus there was no television, no radio or newspapers. People just told each other the news... 'Have you heard...?' and sometimes it got a bit altered as it passed along. You couldn't always believe what you heard.

The two friends of Jesus had heard that he was alive again — but was it really so? They were so busy talking and discussing, so full of their own ideas, that they didn't recognize the truth when it walked *with* them.

Have you noticed how many different ways there are of doing the same thing? At the swimming baths some people dive in like a dolphin, others leap in with a great big splash and some go carefully down the steps — that's me! Mary recognized Jesus when he spoke her name. These two friends recognized Jesus by the way he broke the bread. Then they knew the truth. I bet they wished they'd recognized him sooner!

On these last few days of our Treasure Hunt let's learn to look and listen, for it is then that we will recognize the truth about Jesus.

👉 TO DO

Make the front page of the Jerusalem Times for today. What news will the disciples have to report? Give it a headline about Jesus and draw a 'photograph'. Then write the story (with the important bit in the first sentence, like a proper newspaper).

Behind locked doors

📖 John 20:19–20

It was late that Sunday evening, and the disciples were gathered together behind locked doors, because they were afraid of the Jewish authorities. Then Jesus came and stood among them. 'Peace be with you,' he said. After saying this, he showed them his hands and his side. The disciples were filled with joy at seeing the Lord.

If a hedgehog is frightened he tucks in his little snout and rolls himself into a tight ball so that nobody can come near and hurt him. On the inside his tummy is soft and warm, but on the outside he's a ball of sharp prickles. He's hiding.

Sometimes when we're frightened of what might happen we get a bit 'prickly', too, to stop ourselves from being hurt. Perhaps we shout and get bad-tempered so people will leave us alone. Or we sit on our own and don't join in and they think we're sulky. Just like a hedgehog, we're hiding behind our 'prickles'.

Our door is locked and bolted so that nobody can get in to hurt us — just like that door on Easter Day. But somebody does get in. It's Jesus — the locks and bolts don't stop him. 'Don't be frightened,' he says and he shows us that it is really him. We don't need to be afraid any more.

Wherever we're hiding, behind locked doors or 'prickles', Jesus can find us and make us feel better.

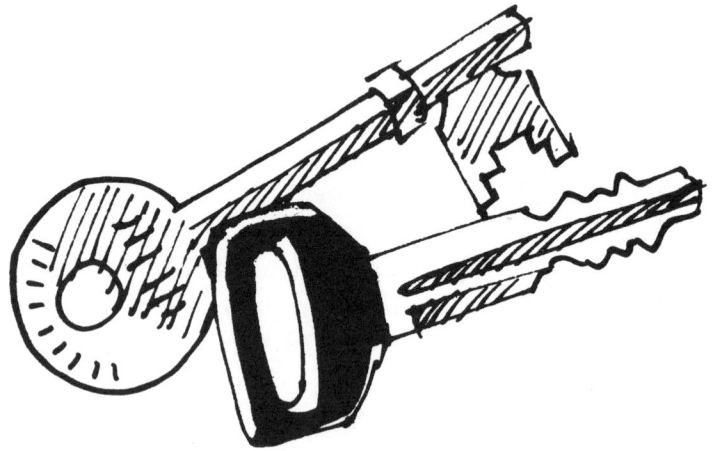

🖐 TO DO

How many keys have you got at home? Front door, back door, perhaps car and garage keys. Ask if you can borrow them just long enough to draw round each one on a piece of paper and write underneath where it comes from. Perhaps you've noticed an old key in your church door, but you must leave that where it is. Now look up Matthew chapter 16 and verse 19 in a Bible. Draw what you think those keys would look like.

Where can I keep this key, Toby?

It's very important and I mustn't lose it.

What's it for?

Er... I've forgotten!

Thomas needs proof

📖 John 20:24–29

One of the twelve disciples, Thomas, (called the Twin) was not with them when Jesus came. So the other disciples told him, 'We have seen the Lord!' Thomas said to them, 'Unless I see the scars of the nails in his hands and put my finger on those scars and my hand in his side, I will not believe.'

A week later the disciples were together again indoors, and Thomas was with them. The doors were locked, but Jesus came and stood among them and said, 'Peace be with you.' Then he said to Thomas, 'Put your finger here, and look at my hands; then stretch out your hand and put it in my side. Stop your doubting, and believe!' Thomas answered him, 'My Lord and my God!' Jesus said to him, 'Do you believe because you see me? How happy are those who believe without seeing me!'

Just imagine being away from school for some reason and returning to find that somebody had paid a surprise visit: a local celebrity, a teacher who once taught there, a TV star. Your friends are all talking about it and at first you think they must *be* joking... then you feel left out.

Thomas was feeling like that — uncertain and left out. And Jesus knew. He came again to that locked room, just for Thomas, and treated him in a special way. And all Thomas' doubts melted away.

Jesus knows that we find it difficult to believe what we cannot see. But look at the leaves dancing on the trees; the corn bowing in a field; the washing flapping on the line. We haven't seen the wind, but we know it's there. We can feel it blowing on our faces. Yes, it's the wind. And in the same way we can believe in Jesus.

☞ TO DO

Draw four large squares on a piece of paper. Each of these 'pictures' is a drawing of something you can't see but which you know is there. Now write underneath what each one is!

A surprise picnic

📖 John 21:7—10

The disciple whom Jesus loved said to Peter, 'It is the Lord!' When Peter heard that it was the Lord, he wrapped his outer garment round him (for he had taken his clothes off) and jumped into the water. The other disciples came to shore in the boat, pulling the net full of fish. They were not very far from land, about a hundred metres away. When they stepped ashore, they saw a charcoal fire there with fish on it and some bread. Then Jesus said to them, 'Bring some of the fish you have just caught.'

There's nothing like a long walk, a bike ride, or an outdoor game, to make you feel hungry. All that fresh air and hard work! And it's a really good feeling — if there's a meal at the end of it. Or maybe you get hungry doing other things.

Peter and his friends were hungry — they'd been out all night fishing. The trouble was, they'd caught nothing... until a man on the shore told them to throw their nets over the other side of the boat. Suddenly... hey presto! More fish than they could cope with. Then they realized the man was Jesus.

What a happy picnic they had. Jesus had come to them again and had given them just what they needed — food. But it was almost time for them to start a different sort of work for him. They would need to do things his way then, just as they'd obeyed him when they were fishing that night.

Have we learned enough about Jesus on our Treasure Hunt to want to do things his way?

👉 TO DO

Make a fishing net like Peter's. Cut a length of string 90 cm long and tie it between two wooden chairs, or the legs of a table. Now cut twenty 60 cm lengths and tie them to the first piece of string to hang down evenly spaced along its length. Knot the lengths together in pairs, about 6 cm down, starting at one end and working along the row. Repeat this, but start with the second string, so that the knotting begins to make a net. Repeat these rows alternately until the net is complete. Cut out some fish shapes, colour them and glue them on to the net. Put a title on it, for example, 'Let's go fishing with Jesus'.

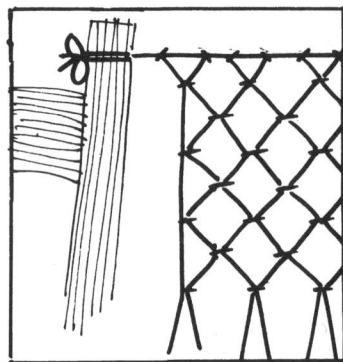

I love barbecues!

Which bit do you like best?

Well, it's either the bit that's burnt or the bit that's not cooked at all!

30

A new beginning

📖 Luke 24:50–53

Then he led them out of the city as far as Bethany, where he raised his hands and blessed them. As he was blessing them, he departed from them and was taken up into heaven. They worshipped him and went back into Jerusalem, filled with great joy, and spent all their time in the Temple giving thanks to God.

Do you like doing jigsaw puzzles? I do. All those little pieces full of knobs — they don't seem to fit at all, but bit by bit the picture **always** comes together. Then that wonderful moment arrives when you slip the last piece into place, sit back, and your picture is complete. Why not try one, an easy one at first?

Our Treasure Hunt has been like a jigsaw puzzle. Although we've enjoyed it there have been things happening that didn't seem to fit, times when we've been puzzled. Some pieces of our puzzle have shown the faces of people Jesus met... some have been a picture of how much he cares... some were sad pictures of when he suffered and died... and then we held a piece in our hand of an empty tomb and Jesus risen from the dead. Today the final piece has been put in place — the picture is complete. Now we know who Jesus is. Jesus is the son of God... everything he did, he did for us. Now we know what love is.

The disciples were too happy to be frightened any more; they didn't need a locked room now. They had things to do for Jesus... and they couldn't wait to begin.

And tomorrow, at last, we will find our Treasure!

👉 TO DO

Write a letter to Jesus. You want to give it to him at Bethany, quickly, before he is taken up into heaven. Tell him which bits of the Treasure Hunt you liked best and how much you will miss him (don't look at tomorrow yet!)
Now slip your letter between the pages of your Bible — Jesus will get the message.

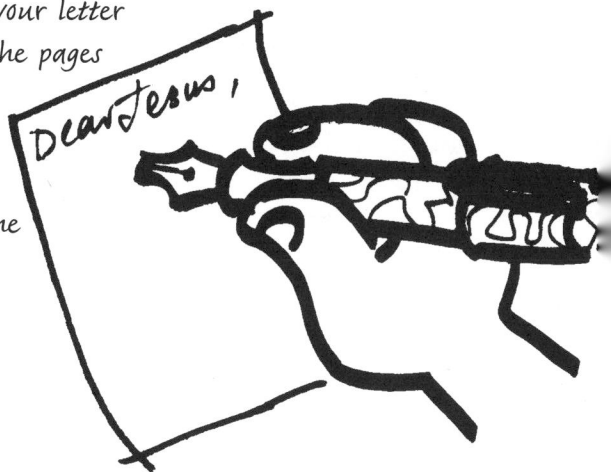

Dear Jesus,

> It's never going to be the same again!

> I shall miss you, Toby! Why do you have to go?

> I'm only moving into my own bedroom!

Our treasure

📖 John 15:12–14 & 17

Love one another, just as I love you. The greatest love a person can have for his friends is to give his life for them. And you are my friends, if you do what I command you... This, then, is what I command you: love one another.

In story-books people go looking for treasure in all sorts of places — desert islands, sunken Spanish galleons, the rainbow's end, even outer space; there are lots of different kinds of treasure.

We have been looking for treasure and we have learned what love is all about as we have travelled with Jesus. Now, at last, we have come to the place where our treasure is. The treasure is just here, wherever you are at this very moment — in a classroom, a car, your bedroom or a garden... wherever you happen to be. Jesus himself is the treasure. Did you know that if there had only been you in the whole world Jesus would still have come so that he could offer you this treasure, this greatest love? Unbelievable but true!

One of the nicest things that can happen to you is when someone asks, 'Will you be my friend?' And Jesus is saying this to you. When you have filled in the word puzzle below you will know what a special friend Jesus will be. And Jesus will never, ever, break his promise to you because he is the treasure which will last for ever.

treasure NOW!

Toby and Trish invite you to rearrange the words in the puzzle, fit them in the grid and discover just what Jesus is promising you.

1	15
3	17
5	19
7	21
9	23
11	25
13	27

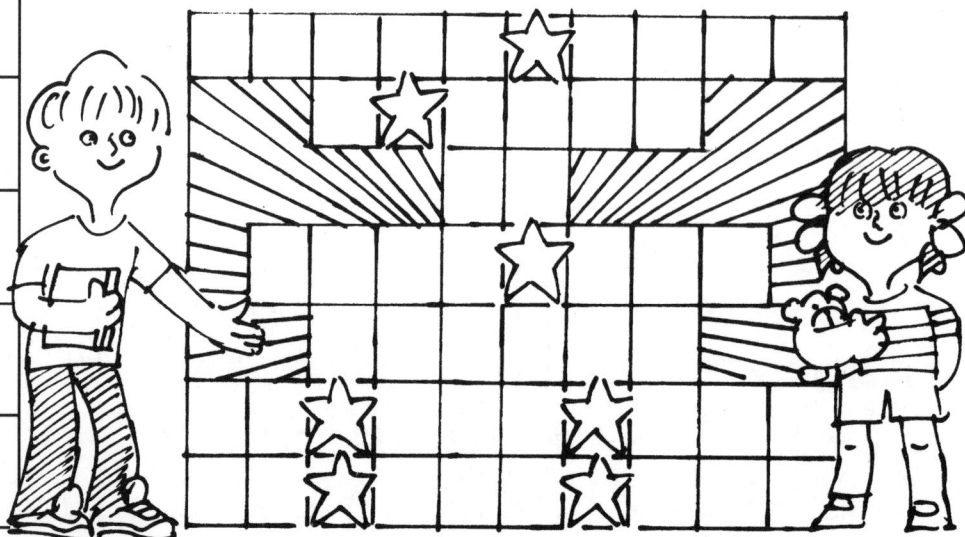

Matthew 28:20

32